ACCOUNTING FOR DEPRECIATION OF NON-CURRENT
ASSETS AND BOOKKEEPING

DEPRECIATION, IMPAIRMENT AND REVALUATION OF
NON-CURRENT ASSETS

ISBN (9781516921997)

INTRODUCTION

It has been glaring that accounting students and business owners are always confused with the appropriate use and calculation of depreciation, impairment, and revaluation of assets.

This book demystifies everything about depreciation of assets, impairment of assets, and revaluation of assets.

This book has been specially prepared for accounting students, business related students and business professionals.

TABLE OF CONTENTS

CHAPTER 1

DEPRECIATION OF NON-CURRENT ASSETS

1.1 Depreciation

Depreciation is the part of a non-current asset that is consumed during its period of use by the business.

IAS 16 describes depreciation as,

"Both the decline in value of an asset over time as well as the systematic allocation of the depreciable amount of an asset over its useful life"

Depreciation is an expense. It needs to be charged to the statement of comprehensive income (Profit and Loss account) as an expense. The amount charged in a year for depreciation will be determined based on the amount of economic usefulness of the asset that is put to use.

Total depreciation over the life of a non-current asset can be calculated simply as cost less the amount receivable when the non-current asset is put out of use by a business entity. This amount receivable is commonly referred to as scrap value or residual value of the asset.

Residual value can be determined based on the current market prices of the asset as at the day of the financial position, and not at the day of original purchase of the asset.

Where a non-current asset is sold within the same accounting period at a price lower than its cost of acquisition, the difference should be charged to the income statement as a provision for depreciation for the period. For example, a non-current asset that was bought for $950, was sold for $450 in the same accounting year. The depreciation to be charged to an income statement for the year will be $950 – 450 =$500

Where a non-current asset is used for more than one accounting period, depreciation should be charged for each accounting period. How then do you allocate depreciation to each accounting period? There are many methods for the calculation and allocation of depreciation. The methods may not give the same result. It is important that the depreciation should be shared over the useful life of each asset.

Non-current assets held for sale

Where non-current assets are regrouped as being non-current assets held for sales, depreciation must not be provided for the assets.

1.2. Causes of Depreciation

Reduction in the value of tangible non-current assets can arise as a result of physical deterioration, economic factors, time and depletion. The following are the causes of depreciation:

Physical deterioration

a) Wear and Tear: When non-current assets such as plant and machinery, fixtures and fittings are being used, they will eventually wear out.

b) Rust, erosion, decay and rot: metal in machinery will rust away. Wood rots.

Economic Factors

These may be the causes of an asset not to be put to use despite the fact that the asset is still in good condition and quality. Economic factors can occur in different ways, such as obsolescence, and inadequacy.

1) Obsolescence: It occurs when an asset is out of date as a result of advancement in technology.

2) Inadequacy: This occurs when an asset is abandoned as a result of its inability to cope with the expansion and growth of the business. This does not mean that the asset is no longer in good condition. For example, a small grinding machine used for producing animal feeds will be inadequate if the business of the animal feeds becomes very big.

Depletion

Some assets are known for wasting nature, probably due to extraction of mineral resources or raw materials from them. Assets such as oil well, and quarries come under this heading. Provision for the consumption of an asset of wasting nature is called provision for depletion.

Reasons for Charging Depreciation are:

1. To know the actual net profit for the period

2. To comply with the matching concepts

3. To know the realistic value of the assets on the statements of financial position

4. To provide funds for assets replacement

1.3 Methods of calculating depreciation charges

There are many methods of calculating depreciation. Some of them are stated below:

1. Straight-line method

2. Diminishing or reducing balance method

3. Sum of the years' digit method

4. Annuity system

5. Sinking fund method

6. Insurance policy system

7. Revaluation method

8. Production unit method

9. Machine Hours method

10. Depreciation fund method

1.4 How to Calculate Depreciation of Non-Current Asset Based on IFRS

IAS 16 states that,

"the depreciation method should reflect the pattern in which the asset's future economic benefits are expected to be consumed by the entity and that appropriateness of the method should be reviewed at least annually in case there has been a change in the expected pattern."

Beyond that, the standard leaves the choice of method to the entity, even though it does cite 'straight-line', 'diminishing balance', and 'units of production' methods.

There are many methods in use for the calculation of depreciation. International Financial Reporting Standards (IFRS) recommends three methods for the calculation of depreciation. They are the straight line, the reducing balance and the units of production method.

1.4.1 Reducing Balance Method or Diminishing Balance Method

In this method, a fixed percentage is written off the reducing balance of the asset account each year after a fixed percentage has been written off the first year cost of the asset.

Reducing balance method can also be referred to as a diminishing balance method.

Illustration 1

If a machine is bought for $20,000 and depreciation is to be charged at 20 per cent, the calculations for the first three years would be as follows:

Solution:

Reducing balance method

		$
Cost		20,000
Less first year depreciation	(20% × 20,000)	-4,000
		16,000
Second year depreciation	(20% × 16,000)	-3,200
		12,800
Third year depreciation	(20% ×12,800)	-2,560
Cost not yet apportioned at the end of year 3		10,240

1.4.2 Straight Line Method

Under the straight line method of depreciation, the cost of acquisition of the asset should be identified. The number of years in which the asset will be put to use should also be identified. The cost is then divided by the number of years. The result is the depreciation charged for each year.

Illustration 1

Machinery was purchased for $50,000 and we estimate that we will put it to use for 6 years and thereafter sold it for $3,500. What is the depreciation charged for each year?

Solution:

$$\text{Depreciation} = \frac{\$50,000 - \$3,500}{6}$$

$$= \$7,750$$

On the other hand, if we believed that after 6years, the asset will not have a residual value, the charge for depreciation will be:

$$= \frac{\$50,000 - 0}{6}$$

$$= \$8,333.33$$

1.4.3 Units of Production Depreciation Methods

The units of production depreciation method is the most accurate and appropriate method of calculating depreciation where the extent and amount of depreciation is determined by the usage of asset during production.

Its use is limited to those assets for which some estimate of production can be attached, but it is a particular choice of those who use activity-based costing systems because it closely relates asset cost to actual activity.

To calculate it, estimate the total amount of expected units of production that can be produced by the asset. The following are the steps to be taken in calculating it:

Step1

Divide the cost of the assets after residual value (cost – residual value) by the expected total units of production to arrive at a depreciation per unit.

Step 2

Multiply the depreciation per unit by the total units of production in a particular accounting period to arrive at the depreciation for the period.

ILLUSTRATION 1

A machine, at an oil company, is assembled at a cost of $700,000. It is expected to be used in the extraction of 2 million barrels of oil, which results in an anticipated depreciation rate of $0.35 per barrel. During the first month, 47,000 barrels of oil are extracted.

What is the depreciation for the period?

SOLUTION:

The depreciation for the month:

= Depreciation per unit of production × total production for the Period

= $0.35 × 47,000 barrels

= $16,450

This calculation also can be used with service hours as its basis rather than units of production. When used in this manner, the method can be applied to a larger number of assets for which production volumes would not be otherwise available.

CHAPTER 2

Double Entry Records for Depreciation

Recording depreciation involves maintaining each non-current asset at its historical cost. Another ledger account where the depreciation to date is recorded is also kept. The account where depreciation to date is kept is called accumulated provision for depreciation account or accumulated depreciation account.

2.0 Double Entry Book-keeping for depreciation:

Debit the statement of comprehensive income (profit and loss account)

Credit the accumulated provision for depreciation account

Example 1

A business has a financial year end of December 31. A computer was bought for $4,000 on January 1, 2008. It is to be depreciated at the rate of 20 percent per annum using the reducing balance method. Record the depreciation on double entry bookkeeping.

Solution:

Calculation of depreciation using reducing balance method

		$
Cost as at Jan. 1,2008		4,000
Depreciation, Dec.31, 2008	20% x 4,000	-800
Balance as Jan. 1,2009		3,200
Depreciation, Dec.31, 2009	20% x 3,200	-640
Balance as Jan. 1,2010		2,560
Depreciation, Dec.31, 2010	20% x 2,560	-512
Balance as at Jan. 1 , 2011		2,048

Computer Accounts

2008		$			
Jan. 1	Cash	4,000			

Accumulated Provision for depreciation A/C

2008		$	2008		$
Dec.31	Balance c/d	800	Dec.31	P&L	800
2009			2009		
			Jan. 1	Balance b/d	800
Dec.31	Balance c/d	1,440	Dec.31	P&L	640
		1,440			1,440
2010			2010		
			Jan. 1	Balance b/d	1,440
Dec.31	Balance c/d	1,952	Dec.31	P&L	512
		1,952			1,952
			2011		
			Jan. 1	Balance b/d	1,952

NOTE:

P&L means profit and loss accounts

Statement of Comprehensive Income
(Profit & Loss Accounts)

2008		$
Dec. 31 Acc. Prov. for depreciation		800
2009		
Dec. 31 Acc. Prov. for depreciation		640
2010		
Dec. 31 Acc. Prov. for depreciation		512

Statements of financial position (extracts)

As at Dec. 31,		
2008	$	$
Computer at cost	4,000	
Accumulated		
Depreciation.	-800	
		3,200
As at Dec. 31,		
2009		
Computer at cost	4,000	
Accumulated		
Depreciation.	-1,440	
		2,560
As Dec. 31, 2010		
Computer at cost	4,000	
Accumulated		
Depreciation.	-1,952	
		2,048

2.1 The disposal of a Non-current Asset

When a non-current asset is sold, we need to remove it from the ledger accounts. This can be done in the following ways:

a) The cost of the asset sold has to be removed from the asset accounts

b) The accumulated depreciation of the asset sold has to be taken out of the accumulated provision for depreciation accounts

c) The profit or loss on the asset sold has to be determined.

Accounting Entries needed are as follows:

The following entries are needed in the sale of a non-current asset:

1. Transfer the cost of the asset sold to an asset disposal account:
Debit asset disposal account
Credit asset account

2. Transfer the depreciation already charged to asset disposal account:
Debit accumulated provision for depreciation account
Credit asset disposal account

3. For the amount received on disposal:
Debit bank or cash account
Credit asset disposal account

3. Transfer the difference (i.e. the amount required to balance the asset disposal account) to the statement of comprehensive income (profit and loss account)

a) If the asset disposal account shows a difference on the debit side (profit):
Debit asset disposal account
Credit profit and loss account

b) If the asset disposal account shows a difference on the credit side (loss):
Debit profit and loss account
Credit asset disposals account

ILLUSTRATION 1

Equipment costing $120,000 was bought on 1ˢᵗ January 2001. Depreciation was provided at 20% annually on straight line method. It was sold on 30ᵗʰ June, 2004 for $31,500.

You are required to calculate:

a) its accumulated depreciation at the time of sales

b) profit or loss in the year of sales

c) the net book value of the asset at the time of sale

Solution:

a) $3.5 \times 20\% \times \$120,000 = \$84,000$

b)

Equipment Disposal Accounts

	$		$
Cost	120,000	Acc. Depn.	84,000
		Cash	31,500
		P&L	4,500
	120,000		120,000

Loss was $4,500 in the year of sales.

	$
c) Cost	120,000
Accumulated depreciation	(84,000)
Net Book Value	36,000

ILLUSTRATION 2

The table below shows information concerning machinery imported from abroad.

	$
Purchase price of machinery	120,000

Import duty	11,000
Installation cost	5,500
Annual maintenance cost	1,400
Estimated useful life 5years	
Estimated scrap value	6,000

a. What is the total acquisition cost of the equipment?

b. What is the annual depreciation charged if straight line method is used?

Solution:

a.

	$
Purchase price of machinery	120,000
Import duty	11,000
Installation cost	5,500
	136,500

b. $\dfrac{136,500 - 6,000}{5} = \$26,100$

2.2. Changes of depreciation Method

It is possible to make a change in the calculation of depreciation. The change should not be frequent. Where a change to the depreciation is material, the effect of the change on the reported figure should be stated as a note to the financial statement in the year of the change.

CHAPTER 3

IMPAIRMENT OF ASSETS

3.0 Impairment of Assets

According to IAS 36, impairment of assets ensures that assets are not carried in the statement of financial position at more than their recoverable amount (i.e the higher of fair value less cost of disposal and the value in use)

IAS 36 applies to the following assets:

1) Land
2) Buildings
3) Machinery and equipment
4) Investment property carried at cost
5) Intangible assets
6) Goodwill
7) Investments in subsidiary, associates and joint venture carried at cost
8) Assets carried at revalued under IAS 16 and IAS 38

IAS 36 does not apply to the following assets

1) Inventories
2) Assets arising from construction contracts
3) Deferred tax assets
4) Assets arising from employees' benefits
5) Investment property carried at fair value
6) Agricultural assets carried at fair value
7) Financial assets
8) Insurance contract assets
9) Non-current assets held for sales

Key definitions are as follows:

3.0.1 Impairment Loss

Impairment loss is the amount by which the carrying amount of an asset in the statement of financial position is higher than the recoverable value of the asset.

3.0.2 Carrying amount

Carrying amount is the amount at which an asset is carried in the statement of financial position after deducting accumulated depreciation.

3.0.3 Recoverable amount

Recoverable amount is the higher of an asset fair value less cost of its disposal and its value in use.

3.0.4 Fair Value

Fair value is the price that would be received to sell an asset or paid to transfer a liability in orderly transactions between market participants at the measurement date.

3.0.5 Value in Use

Value in use is the present value of the future cash flow expected to be derived from an asset or cash-generating unit.

3.0.6 Cash Generating Unit

Cash generating unit is a small group of identifiable assets from which cash inflow is expected.

3.1 How do we find out that there is impairment?

Every company shall watch out for external and internal indicators of a possible impairment.

3.2.1 External indicators are significant decline in market value, significant adverse changes in technological, market, economic or legal environment, increase in market interest rates or rates of return, and carrying amount of company's net assets exceeds market capitalization.

3.2.2. Internal indicators are obsolescence or physical damage, internal evidence available that asset's performance will be worse than expected, significant adverse changes to company including plans to discontinue or restructure an operation using the asset or to dispose of it earlier than planned.

Therefore, if the company finds any of these indicators, it should determine asset's recoverable amount, and find out whether there is impairment.

The recoverable amounts of the following types of intangible assets are measured annually whether or not there is an indication of impairment of assets:

An intangible asset with an indefinite useful life

An intangible asset not yet available for use

Goodwill acquired in a business combination

Case Study 1

Jevta Ltd. has a machinery that amounted to $70,000 after accumulated depreciation as at December 31,2014. It is discovered that there was a decline in the market value of the machinery. The fair value of the asset as at December 31, 2014 was $65,000 and value in use of the asset was $55,000.

You are required to provide answers to the following questions:

1) What is the carrying amount

2) What is the recoverable value

3) Calculate impairment loss

4) Post the information above to journal

5) Record the asset in the statement of financial position

Solutions

1) The carrying amount of the machinery as at December 31 2014 was $70,000.

2) The recoverable value is the higher of the fair value less cost to sale, and the value in use. The fair value ($65,000) is higher than the value in use ($55,000). Therefore, the recoverable value is $65,000.

3)

	$
Recoverable value	65,000
Carrying amount	-70,000
Impairment loss	5,000

4)

Journal Entry

	$	$
Income statement	5,000	
Machinery		5,000

Being the amount recorded for impairment loss

5)
Statement of financial position as at December 31, 2014

	$
Machinery	100,000
Less accumulated depreciation	(30,000)
	70,000
Less impairment loss	(5,000)
	65,000

Note:
We assume that the accumulated depreciation is $30,000.

3.3 How to Account for Impairment Loss

There are two models for accounting for impairment losses:

3.3.1 Cost Model

Debit: statement of comprehensive income

Credit: Asset account

3.3.2 Revaluation Model

Debit: Equity; revaluation surplus

Credit: asset account

Note:

If there is no positive balance figure on revaluation surplus, cost model should be used.

3.3.3 Reversal of Impairment Loss

Where there is an indication that an impairment loss might have been decreased, reversal of the impairment loss under cost model is always recognized.

Accounting entries for the reversal of impairment loss are as follows:

Debit: Asset accounts

Credit: statement of comprehensive income (P&L); Reversal of impairment loss

3.4 Recoverable Value of an Individual Asset and cash Generating Unit

If it is not possible to calculate the recoverable value of an individual asset, then the recoverable amount of the CGU (cash generating unit to which the asset belongs should be calculated. CGU is a small group of identifiable assets that can generate cash inflow for an entity as a continuous use of the assets and are independent of cash flow from other assets.

Any impairment loss calculated for a CGU should be allocated to reduce the carrying amount of the asset in the following order:

- the carrying amount of goodwill should be first reduced, then the carrying amount of other assets of the unit should be reduced on a pro rata basis, which is determined by the relative carrying value of each asset; then
- any reductions in the carrying amount of the individual assets should be treated as impairment losses. The carrying amount of any individual asset should not be reduced below the highest of its fair value less cost to sell, its value in use, and zero.
- If this rule is applied, then the impairment loss not allocated to the individual asset will be allocated on a pro rata basis to the other assets of the group.

Example
A cash-generating unit has the following net assets:

	$m
Goodwill	60
Property	120
Plant	180
	360

A recoverable amount has been determined and is $270.

Allocate the impairment loss to the net asset of the entity.

Solution:

	Goodwill	Property	Plant	Total
	$m	$m	$m	$m
Carrying amount	60	120	180	360
Impairment loss	-60	-12	-18	-90
Carrying value after impairment	0	108	162	270

CHAPTER 4

REVALUATION OF FIXED ASSETS (NON-CURRENT ASSETS)

Revaluation of fixed assets is the process of increasing or decreasing their carrying amount in case of major changes in the market value of the fixed assets.

International Financial Reporting Standards stipulated that fixed assets should be initially recorded at cost, but they allow two models for subsequent accounting for fixed assets, namely cost model and revaluation model.

4.1 Cost Model

Under cost model, fixed assets are carried at historical cost less accumulated depreciation and accumulated impairment losses.

ILLUSTRATION 1

Samotex Ltd. purchased a building worth $100,000 on January 1, 2006. The building has a useful life of 10 years, and the company uses straight line method of depreciation. What will be the value of the building at December 31, 2008 and accumulated depreciation for the period?

Record the above information in the book of accounts.

SOLUTION:

Step 1

The building will first be recorded at its historical cost.

Journal Entry

	Dr.	Cr.
	$	$
Building	100,000	
Cash		100,000

Step 2

The historical cost of the building will be reduced by the accumulated deprecation and accumulated impairment loss of the building.

Calculation of accumulated depreciation:

$100,000/10 = \$10,000$

Annual depreciation $= \$10,000$

Accumulated depreciation as at December 31, 2008:

$3 \times \$10,000 = \$30,000$

The carrying amount is $100,000 minus $30,000 which equals $70,000.

We can see that the building remains at its historical cost and is periodically depreciated with no other upward adjustment to value.

4.2 Revaluation Model

Under revaluation model, an asset is initially recorded at its historical cost, but subsequently adjusted for increase in value to account for any appreciation in value.

The only difference between the cost model and the revaluation model is that cost model only allows downward adjustment due to impairment losses while revaluation model allows both upward and downward adjustment in value of an asset.

ILLUSTRATION 2

Consider the illustration 1 of Samotex Ltd. as stated in case of cost model. Assume on December 31, 2008, the company intends to switch to revaluation model and carries out revaluation exercise which estimates the fair market value of the building to be $90,000 as at December 31, 2008. The carrying amount at the date is $70,000.

      a) What is the amount of upward adjustment if there is any?

      b) What is the revalued amount of the building?

SOLUTION:

a)

The upward amount:
= $ 90,000 - $70,000
= $20,000

b)
The revalued amount of the building is $90,000 because the carrying amount of $70,000 increased by $20,000.

Journal entry

	Dr. $	Cr. $
Building	20,000	
Revaluation surplus		20,000

Being the amount of the revaluation of asset

Note:

Upward revaluation is not considered as a normal gain and is not recorded in the income statement rather it is directly credited to equity account called revaluation surplus. Revaluation surplus contains all the upward revaluation of company's assets until all those assets are disposed off.

4.2.1 Depreciation after Revaluation

Depreciation in the periods after revaluation is based on the revalued amount. Under the illustration of Samotex Ltd., depreciation for 2009 shall be the new carrying amount divided by the remaining useful life or $90,000/7 which is equal to $12,857.14.

4.2.2 Reversal of Revaluation

If a revalued asset is subsequently valued down due to impairment, the loss is first written off against any available balance in the revaluation surplus and if the loss is higher than the balance in the revaluation surplus of the same asset, the difference is charged to the income statement as impairment loss.

ILLUSTRATION 3

Assume (refer to 4.2.1 above) on December 31, 2010 Samotex Ltd. revalues the building again to find out that the fair value should be $60,000.

Carrying amount as at December 31, 2010 is $90,000 minus 2-year depreciation (2×12,857.14) which amounts to $64,285.72.

The carrying amount exceeds the fair value by ($64,285.72 - $60,000) = $4,285.72. The revaluation surplus should be reduced by $4,285.72. The company is already having $20,000 in the revaluation surplus account meant for the same asset. This $20,000 is sufficient to absorb the impairment loss ($4,285.72) and hence, there is no need to post the impairment loss to an income statement.

Journal Entry

	$	$
Revaluation Surplus	4,285.72	
Building Account		4,285.72

REFERENCES:

Frank Wood (12th edition) Business Accounting

Toye Adelaje (2015) Basic Financial Accounting

www.ingramcontent.com/pod-product-compliance
Lightning Source LLC
Chambersburg PA
CBHW072259200526
45168CB00016B/2177